Caring for Souls

Poetry, Prose, Art, and More

Lisa Tomey-Zonneveld

Contributing Author & Editor

Published by Prolific Pulse Press LLC

Lisa Tomey-Zonneveld, Manager prolificpulse@gmail.com

Individual Contributor Poems are subject to First Rights Publication in Caring for Souls unless otherwise indicated.

Library of Congress Control Number: 2022917241

ISBN: 979-8-9863237-7-0 Paperback

Lisa Tomey-Zonneveld, Contributing Author, and Editor

Kay Payne, Cover Artist

to care for cherished souls

reach your hand across your chest

feel the beat of your heart

trust me, my friend

that is all you need

Table of Contents

Dedication

Dedicated to compassionate souls and those who need solace. Sometimes, they are the same.

Previously Published

Acknowledgements

Thank you to all the wonderful poets and essayists who have delve deep into their hearts and brought forth such treasured works. Thank you to Kay Payne for her artistic cover and internal art. Thank you to all the journals who value our submissions. And especially thank you to family, friends, and friends who become like family for always being the cheerleaders.

Introduction

When I embarked on this project, it was going to be solo. For some time, I have been in various care roles, as a giver and receiver. One thing I learned is that there is nothing you can do without others. So I decided it would be more beneficial to open up this book to other writers.

It all began with an appeal or call to others where I ran a contest. The requirements were that each writer had to speak from their own experience. We paid an honorarium to each chosen for publication.

These writers have dug deep into their souls to express their honesty about these experiences. I found it important to keep tissues handy while reading these heartfelt words. Those who know me know I do not cry easily. I frequently choked up. I say this to offer a trigger warning that there are many deeply emotional stories within these writings. It started with an invitational poem by Jill Sharon Kimmelman, followed by the winning submissions. Next, I have a section of my works, some of which have been published in journals and anthologies. There are even comfort food recipes from my family files.

Beyond the writing, it is also important to explore our own stories. The journal and art pages which are placed after the expressions provide this opportunity. When caregivers and receivers are in their spaces, creativity in various art forms can be beneficial. We have been fortunate to have the renderings of our cover artist Kay Payne also within the covers of this book. After the journal, you will find her coloring pages for all ages.

Resources for care are plentiful but can be time-consuming to locate and determine the feasibility. We have provided a simple, not likely exhaustive resource list, found in the last portion of this book.

Thank you for taking the time to read these many thoughtful offerings and may your journey never leave you feeling alone.

This book is written in a large print, workbook sized format to allow for visual clarity and the benefit of plenty of space to write notes.

Lisa Tomey-Zonneveld

Jill Sharon Kimmelman

For nurses everywhere…everyday, everywhere, they are in the front lines of this battle called Corona, our masked dedicated unrecognized heroes.

Written, with gratitude, while I was a hospital patient in appreciation to my exceptional team of nurses.

Double Shift

Another crazy chaotic workday looms, twenty-four-hours
can you do it, perhaps

You must turn a deaf ear to the noisy chatter of concerns
threatening to topple every textbook, fence-post, memorized
statistic inside your bleary mind

It's not a day for dreaming dreams, sipping coffee slowly,
it's a day for getting through under, over out the door

Minute by minute, hour after hour
they call out your name
clinging in corners patients with fears
so many lost souls riddled with grief
their red-rimmed eyes swimming with tears

Anxious patients wait, not always patiently
pressing, re-pressing, pounding their buttons
you cannot ignore those incessant bells

Needy people needing you
each one demanding something different

A break, a meal, a hug, change for the bus
chatter turns to shouting, demands soar, lines swell
fighting against their dying
headed for heaven, they are scared, you are too
face it, some days are just plain hell!

They need you to take them outside their confusion
miles away from their pain
Thirteen hours to go, welcome back hero
to the frenzy, to the chaos, to the tiny spark of
someone's hope

Do they say the words aloud
or is it enough just to see thanks in their smile
on a face that hasn't smiled in perhaps a dozen years?

So many sounds, too many sounds
by day's end you are ready, more than ready for silence
when it comes it is too quiet
you lay restless engulfed in dark stillness
sleep has become your unanswered prayer

You realize then, it hits you hard
you have not heard that cherished voice all day

When at last you make the call, she is half-asleep
words are soft
you clutch them to you as a prize
finally now you can close your eyes

You helped a few souls, fought the good fight
another workday fades to black
as she enters your dreams beautiful in resplendent light.

October 2019

From: *You Are The Poem*
Published November 2021

Jill Sharon Kimmelman has been twice nominated for the Pushcart Prize. Recent publications include *Vita Brevis Press, Spillwords Press, Fine Lines, Love of Food,* and multiple anthologies. She has published *You Are the Poem,* a three-themed debut collection of poetry, art, and photography, November 2021. Passions: Reading aloud, cooking, photography, and theatre. She lives in Delaware USA with her husband Tim and is the proud mother of her son Jordan.

Sarfraz Ahmed

Lean On Me

I wish I was strong enough to heal the pain,
The pain inflicted again and again,
Release the tubes that connect the brain,
The oxygen cylinder,
That makes your lungs flare up and let go.
I wish I could carry you,
To wherever you need to go,

So, hold onto me,
I'll carry the weight upon my shoulder,
Upon my spine,
Put your body next to mine,
Lean on me,
And I will wrap my wings around you,
I'll carry the weight upon my shoulder,
The way a mother holds her young,
Lean on me and I promise to be strong.

Sarfraz Ahmed lives and works in the East Midlands, UK. His published books include poetry debut *Eighty-Four Pins – Poetry Collection* (June 2020) and *My Teachers an Alien!* (November 2020). *Two Hearts – A Journey into Heartfelt Poetry* (February 2021) with Annette Tarpley and *Stab the Pomegranate – Collective Poetry* (August 2021).

Nanci Arvizu

Time Travel Care

When a friend asked if I would care for her after a two-for-one surgery, I jumped at the chance.

Having recently moved across the country to be closer to her offspring and their growing family, (otherwise known as Grandkids!) she didn't have anyone close to her that could be that close to her - in those intimate moments of recovery. Not that we'd ever been that intimate, but as friends, at least we could be comfortable in the uncomfortable.

The two for one surgery was for a damaged rotator cuff and a torn bicep. Her shoulder started hurting during the move. The picking, packing, boxing, and carrying that lasted for months took its toll, especially on a body that thinks she can do it all by herself. Thought no woman ever.

She considers the torn bicep one of those 'adding insult to injury' type things. It happened with the last box she moved. The very last one.

It took her a few months to get settled in her new state and home and work on the details of health insurance, doctors, and schedules. When she had her surgery date, she called and asked if I could come for 10 days.

"How about 2 weeks," I offered. "I'll come a few days early to get the lay of the land and then add 2 days in the end, just to be sure you're okay. Because once I'm on the airplane, you're on your own."

Going from the high desert of Arizona to the rolling hills of Virginia is a beautiful shock to the system. Arriving days after one of the worst snowstorms the area had seen in recent memory, added another element to the adventure. Driving on roads with black ice wasn't something I had thought of when I said yes, but fortunately, the ice melted quickly. The snow stuck around making what was already a storybook pretty into a magical wonderland. And I was driving an F-350. I felt like I owned the road even if it was at 10 miles an hour.

I settled into the extra-large bedroom over the garage and fell in love with the view of the lake out the window over the antique desk set up for me to use. I took pictures and sent them to my cousin with the message, "I could write a book here."

The internet had not been a problem prior to the storm. In the hours between the storm and my arrival, it got spotty. In the days between my arrival and before the surgery, it did not improve. We did our own testing, removed devices, played with the television, and did all the things we could think of to improve the connection. No matter what we did we made didn't make enough of a difference - I couldn't access my classwork. Calls to the local internet provider didn't give us much hope. They weren't working to fix the lines. Instead, they were installing a new broadband service which would be up and running within a few weeks. In the meantime, everyone was just going to have to live with the spotty service.

On the day of the surgery, I found a local library and made great use of their wi-fi. I used up almost all of my available late passes for assignments then emailed instructors, colleagues, and friends to let everyone know I was going to be off-line for a while.

For a few days I kept trying to log on, but it wasn't working. I finally convinced myself it was okay. I was okay, and the world would be okay if I wasn't online. The important people in my world knew where I was and what was happening.

Not being connected to the outside world meant being present without distractions and time for long conversations about things, all the things, everything. The ability to have deep, meaningful conversations is becoming a lost art. We hardly even pick up the phone anymore to make an actual phone call! We talked about the oddities of this future world we're living in and the oddity of those who don't want to keep up with it. And the oddest thing of all, this growing old thing.

We laughed about how this way of living was like 'being back in the 80s,' when technology was something we thought only happened at places like the phone company or NASA. Fortunately, we were able to download movies, like it was the 90s, and watch them like VHS tapes from Blockbuster. Pause and rewind with no commercials.

Without a schedule of classes, meetings, and things to do that kept me glued to a screen, the shoulder and bicep healing nicely, the snow melting, and the sun out and about in big blue skies, we got out of the house a little more than we expected. Driving along rolling hills lined with expansive farms, fields or forests, and neighborhoods both old and new, there were moments when I'd catch myself driving like my grandmother - slowing to nearly a stop to point at something, an old farmhouse, a barn, or an abandoned building - like I'm an out-of-towner-lookie-looer. Which I was.

We drove out to a vineyard and had lunch with a sampling of white wines. My friend signed up for their wine club. Then we discovered an A-list celebrity-owned a home nearby and decided to see if we could find it, which took us through more of those beautiful rolling hills of Virginia. The house we found wasn't behind a gate which made us question if our celebrity really owned it. But it didn't matter, the drive was totally worth it.

Hearing my friend's stories of her childhood and young adulthood was a walk through time, for both her and me. She shared things about her loves, her parents, siblings, marriages, children, and the work of her life. The highs and lows and how they all seem to even out in the end. And when you get to the time in your life when there are more years behind you than ahead of you how your perspectives have a way of changing.

We talked about the people in our lives, mostly. The ones who had left their marks on us, good and bad. How tiny decisions could have huge and lasting impacts. And what it feels like to finally be free of such things, otherwise known as learning from our mistakes.

There were talks about culture, beliefs, politics, and history. Discussions about the future included neuroplasticity, skincare and what it might be like to live in a retirement village where everyone drives golf carts and the hottest ticket around is for the 4 pm seating for dinner at the clubhouse.

On the serious side, we talked about aging. The weird things an aging body does and the ways we try to fix it or work with it, depending on our level of tolerance. After a Sunday morning spent being entertained and enlightened at a Drag Queen brunch, we realized there are always wigs and mimosas. And roller skates. Don't forget the roller skates.

The workers were still busy putting the broadband cables into the earth alongside the roads when my caregiving journey sadly came to an end. My friend had been given the all-clear to move on to physical therapy and the most important part, to drive. I was no longer needed. For the physical part anyway.

We enjoyed each other's company and agreed her healing had a lot to do with how much fun we had during her recovery. I admitted to having felt 'healed' too; I could not remember a time when I had laughed so often and watched so many goofy movies in a row. It was like I'd spent a super long weekend at a friend's house, being kids again.

I'd like to thank the internet for not being present during this time.

It kind of makes me miss the 80s.

 **Nanci Arvizu** is an author, speaker, podcaster, and tech lover with nomadic dreams. Poetry and essays published in *A Safe and Brave Space* (2021), *Fine Lines Journal* (2021), *Social Justice Inks* (2022), and *Speak Magazine* (2022). Fiction & non-fiction e-books are available on Amazon.

Kathy Jo Bryant

Timothy*

Timothy was a special guy,
And he had many a friend.
He loved to help with many jobs,
His memories are without end.

He had lots of favorite things,
Pencils were high on his list.
A notebook full of school stuff,
Was loved and would be missed.

His drumsticks, he called, strumsticks,
And he could use them, too!
If you would sing along with him,
You'd be a part of his crew!

He loved to work and split the wood,
And knots he'd split right through!
If told to go around them,
He'd say, "Me split'em," that he'd do!

He was born a challenged soul,
But he was special, too.
His family treated him as the rest,
Tim stuck to them like glue.

Many folks are just like Tim,
Please love them as your friend.
They'll love you back, Oh, yes they will,
And forever, without end!

*My husband's younger brother.
I was his caregiver for a number of years.
He was Downs. He also had Alzheimer's,
and a seizure disorder.

First published in *Poetree.* October 26, 2020

Kathy Jo Bryant hails from Missouri, USA. She is the author of: *Golden Glowing Mushroom, Favorite Things in My World.*

Her work is in a growing number of published anthologies. She is a member of, and former moderator for, the growing Facebook poetry group: The Passion of Poetry.

Mike Dailey

My Pessimistic Wife

My pessimistic wife wants to put me in a bubble

With my platelet count the way it is

she's predicting naught but trouble

She took away my razor; she's hidden my nail clippers

She won't let me go barefoot; she doesn't trust my slippers

I think she's thinking steel toes and a suit of armor suit

A helmet for my head then a place where I'll take root

The roses – no, the whole outside; she considers them quite deadly

If I should prick my finger; will I become a dead me

With Band-Aids in her pocket, she watches like a hawk

Points out all the obstacles each time I stand to walk

She's probably thinking padding for my elbows and my knees

I can't take much more of this won't someone stop her please

Sure my platelet count is down some; but hardly under par

I'm not a hemophiliac; nothing's gone that far

I'd have to prick an artery for there to be a geyser

Someone needs to sit her down; talk to her – advise her

I know that her intentions are as noble as can be

But this all day long attention will be the death of me

Who Is this Woman

They said it was cancer, they said they were sure
My wife took it hard but said we'd endure
She'd take care of me she said with a smile
And I kind of like her warm nursing style

Who is this woman I'm living with now?
She looks like my wife but she's different some how
She's warm and affectionate; I'm thinking "WOW!"
Who is this woman I'm living with now?

Who is this woman that's acting so strange?
I thought such niceness was out of her range
Don't get me wrong, I'm loving the change
Who is this woman that's acting so strange?

Who is this woman who wants to hold hands?
Who hugs me and tells me that she understands
Who somehow became one of my biggest fans?
Who is this woman who wants to hold hands?

Who is this woman who's giving me kisses?
Each morning and evening now, she never misses
She wants to fulfill all my wants and my wishes
Who is this woman who's giving me kisses?

Who is this woman, I must be precise
I've lived with this woman 2/3 of my life
Through sickness and health, through good times and strife
Who is this woman? – It must be my wife.

Mike Dailey is a fairly well known poet in southeast North Carolina. He lives near Sunset Beach with his wife of 50 years and the occasional visits with his daughter and two grandkids. His poems have been published in several magazines and anthologies. He has had three books of poetry collections published; one based on cancer treatments he underwent, one based on his 30 years working as a civilian analyst for the US Army, and a book of spiritual poems. He is currently putting together several collections and looking for a publisher. Mike Dailey's poetry can be serious, topical, or very moving but he is known more for his rhythm and rhyme poetry with a twist of humor.

Christine M. Du Bois

A Question of the Brain

For over a decade,
I've cooked and scrubbed and spooned and smiled
to keep mice away
and her crumbly body comfortable,
and her mood amiable—
or at least moderated—
and for over a decade
I've brought her treats and decorated for holidays
and changed her diapers,
and every day now
I launder leaked urine out of bed pads
and nightgowns. I wish
I could launder leaked urine clear out of
my mind. Still, this is all OK—
compassion propels me—
until our lately daily
dose of paranoia.
At six o'clock she thanks me
for cutting her pasta into tiny pieces.
She forgets I also cleaned all the counters,
and took out the trash,
and sang her favorite songs.

But that's OK. This is where dementia
has led her. Tonight unusually,
she compliments my clothes.
Then suddenly, though not unusually,
at 6:10 she's sure—unshakably convinced—
that I'm there to harm her.
That I find that fun.
That the pasta is poisoned.
That diapering is a prelude
to premeditated death.
It goes on and on, for hours.
And she's mistaken:
unmistakably then, she's not at all fun.
I have only one life. Tonight
I admit to myself:
this isn't how I want to spend it.
She imagines we've imprisoned her—
but who is the prisoner? Maybe my compassion
makes *me* the prisoner, loudly ambushed
by a jailer repeatedly demeaning
my efforts and my ethics.
She's so creative and skilled
at breathtaking accusations. She hangs onto them
with rock-solid certainty. Why is there never
breathtaking appreciation?
Why do I put up with this?
Why does compassion make me keep helping her?

It's a strange power, compassion is.
It can take over the brain.
And why does she have no idea
how stressfully she affects us?
I know, I know, the answer is dementia,
a deranged brain.

But tonight inside me
I feel reverberations—
an unnerving, questioning refrain,
uncertain,
and previously unheard:
Of our two brains—
hers and mine—
whose is most mysterious,
constraining,
and arguably absurd?

Christine M. Du Bois is an anthropologist of immigration, race relations, and agriculture. She has published three books, as well as poems in over a dozen online literary magazines and print anthologies. Her work explores ecology, social justice, history, and interpersonal themes, including dementia care.

Richard Fireman

Hippocrates Resurrected

We should all be doctors
in spirit. We do not have to practice
the medical arts, fix broken bones,
heal the sick and dying. No. But
the first rule, always, is
to do no harm. When we act,
when we even speak, when
we even look into another's eyes
it should be not only without malice
but with compassion. There is
another you, or I, or they. There is
someone. Someone who has lived
and felt pain as well as joy, someone
who has struggled through the web of life
not knowing where and when the spider
will strike. It may be in the corner
but it is there. It may not be there
but the fear of it is under the covers
always. A gentle voice,
a gentler look can go a long way
to calm the overbeating heart.
A gentle touch can fill the blood with music.

Trust is Learned

Each day is different for us.
Not her. The wheel keeps turning
and arrives where it began.

I say I have a surprise for her
to get my mother to eat.
It's only apple sauce but it works
because to her everything is a surprise.

I think about my mom while driving
and find myself at a stop.
The light changes and I can't remember
if I'm supposed to turn.
I decide to follow my instincts
like she does now instead of thinking.
My surprise is that it works.

My lesson is when I think too much
I take for granted what it brings,
think it is all I have.
It is true I have this bridge
but I have to remember not to forget
it is connected to the rock I build on,
from and to the tethering heart.

The Space in the Air is There

The trees cycle into fall
in blazing red. My mother
is all gray. At the nursing home
her TV shows black&white
like when I was a child,
like she is now. The world
she sees is framed in static.
When I move away from her chair
she forgets I am there.

Just beyond her periphery
the world awaits.
I tell her my wife couldn't make it today.
I don't know when she can, but tell her
she will visit tomorrow. She nods.
After all, it is always tomorrow.

When You Look Too Close It All Blurs

She does not know why she does not know,
why she calls her nurse by her mother's name,
why she no longer hates her mother
now that she needs one again.

Now I am her mother now she's a child
her dreams of me gone to forever,
gone like her mind to a place more unsettled,
where age death & terror are on the other side:
she is turning into her dream.

We rented her first video: *Apollo 13*.
I am reading *Lost Moon* and *Einstein's Dreams*.
My coffee mug is from Cape Canaveral
and has a rocket on it with my name.
I remember as a child wanting to be a scientist
before I knew what it was all about, before
I knew my limits. I remember wanting to go to space
before I knew what was out there,
what wasn't. Now I limit my space travel
to books, watch the heroes on the screen.
My new father's son who works for NASA
told me there's no more SETI project,
no more money for probes of the planets,
no more tries to see if God's out there.

When I went back that night I saw searchlights beaming
as though searching for the lost stars in the sky.

When I got the call I was wearing a T-shirt
of Pink Floyd, picture of a face screaming
dating back to their days with Syd Barrett
now in & out of asylums,
back to the days of Atom Heart Mother.
I still remember seeing their concert
on the Isle of Wight in the '70 summer
under an open starstrewn sky,
giant gong & choir & in the end
blue & gold rockets crisscrossing the night
saying goodbye to earth & hello to forever.

Waiting till the summer to bury the dog,
waiting till the madness to take care of my mother:
life is a series of uneven parallels,
inexact geometries from which we try to learn.

Trying to write while mowing the lawn
motion breaks up what I try to put down,
letters as scrambled as my mother's mind.
When I try to dictate into the recorder
the noise of the machine drowns out the message.
Everywhere there are obstacles, hurdles & changes,
everywhere glaciers in the midst of the sea.

Spring is the appearance of the sun in the air
making us forget about the poison ivy.

I dreamt I was standing on a dock
waving my mother's mind goodbye
fading, fading into the horizon
where she doesn't know who she is
where there is no I
like the ocean blending into the sky.

The Shadow Knows

She holds her head in her hands
as though trying to stop anything more from falling out.
Once in a while she gathers strength
and pushes at her brow,
striving to remember where she is
and who.

Today she was doing better.
It was beautiful outside so we didn't have to talk
about anything inside
like whether she wanted to leave life.

One day she thought she saw an old woman
we thought might be her mother.
There is no more time now
for anything but time
and soon even that will be gone.
There is no death here
but its shadow is everywhere.

Each time her mom
comes a little bit closer.
Each time the other side
is not so far away.
One day there'll be no reason
for my mother to stay here.
One day she'll go over
over there to stay.

Sometimes words emerge from hiding.
I ask her if she's outside and she answers:
"outside, inside, what's the difference?"
There are always ways that we can block the sun.

Richard Fireman has been writing for over fifty years and has given readings at several libraries, Barnes & Noble, and the Colts Neck Fair. He has had almost a hundred poems published in the *Monmouth Review*, five in Collage, two in the International Journal of Poetry Therapy, one in *Passager* magazine, and two in *East Meets West*. In 2009 he contributed a chapter to the book *Writing Away the Demons*, a compendium of thirteen writers' stories of how each of them used writing to deal with life crises, edited by poetry therapist Dr. Sherry Reiter. A collection of his poetry, *Constellations*, is scheduled to be published by Prolific Pulse Press LLC in December 2022.

Chyrel J. Jackson

Unwinding Hands of Time

Time for the caregiver takes on a different sequence.
Time to prepare meals.
Time to administer medications.
Time to assist with baths and showers.
The constant clicking of the clock turning long days into
sleepless hours.
Time to schedule Dr.'s visits and appointments.
Time to rub in lotions and medicated ointments.
If only we could unwind and set back the hands of time.
Before sickness and unkind days can make us change our
minds.
If only we could go back in time before illness changed all
of our lives.
Time to cry in secret.
Time to worry.
Time to pray.
Time to forgive those who wronged us before we face
Judgement day.
Time for the caregiver takes on a different sequence.
No time for rest the caregiver's weary consequence.
If only we could go back in time.
Turn back the hands of time
long before illness changed all our lives.

Longing to Sing Like Sarah Vaughan

I couldn't bridge our gaps or right our wrongs.
I didn't have a Whitney Houston voice to sing
you love songs.
In your time of need to care for you as best
I could, I didn't remember all the pain you
caused in life, I remembered your good.
I wished you never became sick, I wished
you were never ill.
Stage four prostate cancer that spread to
the bones
My God, sobering still.
If only our days were longer
why couldn't we try just a
little harder.
Now our tomorrow's with you
are lost, living on past
memories of you the rest of our forever.
Chilling lasting thoughts of you as
you departed life,
Did you remember Tony or mommy the woman you
called wife?
I wished I could have bridged our gaps and
righted all our wrongs.
Why didn't God give me a voice to sing my dying
Father Sarah Vaughn jazz and blues songs....

Healing Hands

I discovered healing hands in those of my capable
parents.
Leaning in to linger a little longer in maternal hands
that provided the right amount of comfort.
Bruised knees, and other childhood injuries
required the know-how of paternal healing hands.
No one sang like dad as he bandaged cuts, and
scrapes.
Never acknowledging your klutz or clumsy smiling
as he said it's all better now suga-puddin'
lookin' great.
Skateboard accidents, and bicycles that coasted
too fast steeply downhill.
Skinny brown legs with knobby knees now bear
tattooed scars of chasing youthful thrills.
Life brings about swift and cataclysmic changes.
I pray for God's mercy as he places my father in my
Middle-aged, unsure, and feeble hands.
I bring him warm blankets and read to him at
bedside with hot and tasty beverages.
God, please give me strength to care for dad
the way he cared for me.
Please give me loving, and healing hands to be the best
caregiver that my father needs.

Chyrel J. Jackson is an avid lover, reader, and writer of African American Literature. She grew up in a Southern Suburb of Chicago, IL. Influenced by the Literary works of James Baldwin, Toni Morrison, Maya Angelou, Langston Hughes, Nikki Giovanni, and Sonia Sanchez, Jackson writes in the Spirit of these ancestors. Giving a voice to social issues that plague our modern time.

Along with her sister, Lyris D. Wallace, they published *Mirrored Images* and *Different Sides of the Same Coin*, a modern collage of poetry as experienced from the Black female perspective of 2 sisters and authors. This work is an interesting twist on Harlem Renaissance revisited as it collides with 2021 social struggle and unrest of our current time.

Jackson has written Political Opinion Editorials, Book Reviews, Journaling, and Poetry - her first choice of genre. You can find her on Sistersrocnrhyme.com

JeanMarie Olivieri

Care Give and Take

When I take my mother to the doctor
it is hard to know which of us is the patient

She on a walker, me on canes
we jostle, joke, bicker

Alzheimer's meant selling her cozy home
and buying a house with room for me

We've had our difficulties
and we still push and pull

She says, I *can live on my own just fine*
I say, *OK* or just wait it out

She says, *Don't leave me*
I say, *I'm not going anywhere*

She says, *I'm not going to one of those places*
I clench to stifle a response

because someday she will go
my body unable to manage hers

That day is coming soon enough
The caretaker needs a caregiver

Mom loses words and comprehension
I lose my patience and temper

She is the wood rotting
I am the wood being whittled

All that's left will be
sawdust and shavings

JeanMarie Olivieri was a business writer but now mostly writes poetry. She has been published in more journals and anthologies than she has fingers including the NCPS's *Pinesong*. She is a co-organizer for Living Poetry and was co-editor of the *Heron Clan Poetry Anthology* series. jeanmarieolivieri.wordpress.com/

Lauren Salkin

Glitchy Kidneys
And other off-kilter stuff

Nothing's working right.
My father's kidneys empty in the wrong direction.
A kidney fail! His organs floating;
his brain barely bobbing.

Dementia, can't ya understand?
He's not crazy.
He's just underwater.
Every thought is a message in a bottle.

Garbage in; garbage out.

Limp word salad at a dessert buffet.
I don't want it.
Give me mint chocolate chip ice cream any day.

Scoop it! Drop it!
Make that three!--melting into a minty mess;
pie crumbling,
cake flaking,
everything's falling apart on the plate
on a table set for an asylum.
The forks in repose where the spoons should be.

Nothing fits.
The tablecloth is split at the seams,
peek-a-boo food staring back at you
through a precipitous tear,
hanging into the space below your knees onto the floor.

No rugs rectangular, round, or oval.
Just humdrum linoleum,
slippery and dumb,
shoes skidding on chocolate sauce.

I bop my head on the crack that broke my mother's back;
my brain fizzles like fizzy pop,
spritzing nonsense.

I can't find a distant point.

Every time I move forward, I leave something behind—a
younger self with a father who doesn't have to pray before he
pees.

I should feel happy—he's alive at 95–and yet I take things for
granted.
My parents are still parenting.
My 91-year-old mother barely caring for her 95-year-old spouse;
they have each other.

Too many people have nothing,
and I have an abundance of stuff:

emotional, material.
Stuff I don't think about: clothes and shoes.
Too much stuff I have to give up.

Old clothes and shoes I donate to Goodwill for people who don't have enough.

People who don't take things for granted as I do.

I don't know what it's like not to have anything. I'm spoiled and live in a country with far too much.

We have too many things that many people don't have—all of it we take for granted like shoes and kidneys.

Peeing is a privilege.

Now take your Goddamn shoes off the table.

Lauren Salkin: Dysfunctional, wife, mother, and loser of stuff. Making sense out of chaos.

Writer of humor, satire, poetry, and thought pieces. Published work has appeared online and in print. *Huffington Post, Extra Newsfeed, Literally Literary, Muddyum, The Haven,* as well as *ByLine,* and *Shroud Magazine.*
medium.com/@laurensalkin

Pratibha Savani

Well Covered

No one can prepare you
For looking after a loved one
The intensity
The emotions
The juggling
The time
All mashed up inside
While you try and survive
Especially for end of life
When you can't just sit and hide
But to be there
In every way
Sleepless nights
Not eating right
It can take a toll
For everyone
As you battle it out
With your emotions
Preparing for what may come next
Ringing doctors
End of life care

Ensuring the care package is in place
Ensuring your loved one is safe
Ensuring you have covered it all
In order to get the help
However big or small

and life went on....

it feels like a lifetime ago
but in fact, it was only months
since caring for my mum
became a need
we all helped
from my brother
dad and me
we were there
til the end
we didn't know when
but we all knew
that day would come
in the meantime
we spent time with her
helped her
supported her needs
and her medication
cooked her meals
with her dietary requirements
we were figuring it out
how to adjust
to live
and to care
for our mum
during those summer months

when everything felt surreal
and life went on....

Pratibha Savani is a UK Poet, Artist, and author of *Tangles + Knots*. Published in *Open Door Magazine* and in several anthologies, she is a creative soul, inspired by the cosmos, nature, and spirituality. Pratibha likes to defy the rules with her inventive expressions on instagram and facebook: Pratibha Poetry Art.

Lisa Tomey-Zonneveld
My Sister

Four years older than me, my sister was a powerful influence on my life. I looked up to her and wanted to be like her. She was the extrovert to my introvert, which gave each of us a space to be content, but close. She did not always want her younger sister tagging along, but we were autonomous from an early age. After we each did our own activities, we liked to share about our day when we would go to bed. We always shared a big double bed and giggled ourselves to sleep.

My sister grew up earlier than planned, getting married at 15 before we moved away, leaving her with her new husband. It was not long before she came to California to be with us, leaving a mess behind. I was so grateful to have her back with me. We caught up on a lot and I found out that she had the mettle I did not realize.

So, life moved on, she married again and had two children, a boy and girl, who I have always loved and would often spend time with. It was as if we shared in their care, which I enjoyed. What really struck me was her tenacity. She left her husband and started over again, two children in tow, and somehow she made it work.

She started working at an auto parts store. For a woman, this was an unusual position. No surprise that she was running the store like the boss she was. When customers would call to ask about parts, they asked to speak to her. She knew her stuff. It would cause jealousy amongst the male workers, but her boss took it in stride. She was his asset.

Her final marriage brought a daughter into the world. While the marriage did not last, that was the last time she would go down that road. I think it took a lot for a single mom to take the stand she did and to make a life for her family. As you may tell, by now, I admired her strength.

The hardest part was yet to come when her son was killed in an accident. While I know her heart was in the greatest of pain, do you know she said she had a peace come over her when she knew he has passed? She wrote a poem dedicated to him and she read this poem at his service.

Eventually, my sister came to find she had congestive heart failure and ended up on disability. She had no physical strength to keep up the pace of even a desk job. There was a treatment regimen, all this time raising her youngest into adulthood. She did it. She knew her resources. Also, she always looked for ways to be of service to others. On her better days, she would cook up batches of soup she called "Buckets of Love" and deliver them to people in need of a hot meal. On her harder days, she rested until she got another wind. That was one amazing woman.

Around nine years ago, she came to live in North Carolina, after living in the Midwest for several years. Her girls were raising their own families, and both lived away from the Midwest. She had the idea of taking care of some health issues and then moving to Alaska to be with her daughter's family.

Her health issues were a broken ankle and lung cancer. Somehow, she amazingly drove to our home. She started a series of care, including lung surgery. She needed ankle surgery but was too physically weak to handle it. But she trooped it out with the boot and managed well.

She wanted to have her own small apartment, and I completely understood. After securing a place, it was time to get it ready and then proceed with her cancer treatments. We set out to Durham to the Duke Cancer Center, where she completed radiation therapy. This included several trips and a misunderstanding (call it her hope and mine) that she would not need chemotherapy. That was not the case.

Round two was to embark on the chemo journey. All the meds helped her a lot, and she could get the rest she needed. Back pain was a constant, but she got through it, thanks to pharmaceuticals and faith. My daughter was the other trooper as she provided her room for the time when sister needed to stay with us until safe to be alone. She also helped her aunt with whatever she needed.

My sister eventually was well enough to make the trip to Alaska after her cancer doctor told her she would die of something else long before cancer. Sister moved to Alaska and stayed until time for the weather change when she could fly back out. She moved to Iowa and eventually passed away. It was hard for her to talk as her voice was weak and she had coughing from congestion, but I had a phone call from her and we kept in touch with texts and emails.

It took a village to help my sister get better and to help her have quality time while in her last years.

Lisa and Paula

Paula Tomey Allen

When she left, I had a dream. She was on the side of the road at a stand where she was giving away cookies to travelers. That was so much like her. What a force, what a soul, what a blessing to have her in our lives.

Daddy and Me

a mere shadow to his girth, I would hope to be
as smart as him, as strong—as his heart was full
as sensitive, as wise, a purveyor without
judgement, but praise, tactfully conveyed
so that possibility outran low confidence
when at night, we lounged, watching tv,
his Camel blown away from myself,
I nestled into his side; it was that side I sought
whenever I needed to sort out the ways
of this daunting world.

We were not without conflict
as my hormones raged—a tween, then a teen
but he always made sure he watched over me
even when I shooed away his opinions,
he knew I heard him
much later, it was by some cruel fate
mother claimed her crown
and I needed to be daddy's confidante
we picked up, as before, honesty prevailed
and let life be what it would be.

The last time I walked on the ship USS NC BB 55
was in 2004, the last time I saw him in his military glory
three years later, he would move on
claim his heavenly home
and I still feel him close by my side.

Previously Published in *Not Just Anybody Can Be Dad: A Tribute to Fathers* (2022) published by Busta Word Publishing LLC

Max Tomey

Daddy's Favorite Dessert – Mom's Bread Pudding

1 cup cubed bread
2 tablespoons melted butter
1 egg slightly beaten
¼ cup sugar
¼ teaspoon salt
½ teaspoon vanilla
¼ teaspoon cinnamon
2 cups milk, scalded
½ cup raisins OR ¼ cup chocolate chips
Oven 350° F
Combine sugar, salt, vanilla, butter, cinnamon, and egg. Add milk, slowly, stirring constantly. Add bread and raisins or chips. Bake in a 2 quart casserole dish for 45 minutes. Best when served warm.

Note: you can use raisin bread instead of adding raisins. This is a great way to use up bread and a low cost recipe.

Serve with Vanilla Sauce (recipe to follow)

Vanilla Sauce (optional)

2 cups water
1 cup sugar
2 tablespoons flour
2 tablespoons butter
1 teaspoon vanilla
¼ teaspoon salt

Combine sugar, salt, & flour. Boil water. Bring to a low boil and add dry ingredients to the water, stirring constantly. Cook at the low boil for 8 minutes. Remove from heat and add butter and vanilla, stirring well. Cool at room temperature, then cover and refrigerate. Serve over bread pudding.

When daddy would come visit, this was one of the desserts I made often.

Mom

1988 I was just sitting in the living room of married student housing when I got a call. It was my father. After going through so many health emergencies, they diagnosed mother with lung cancer. This being my first real personal experience with cancer, I got off the phone, after getting details (not much yet) and sat down, sliding to the floor on my knees and begging for a miracle. What kind of cruelty is this to heap upon a woman who knew too much pain in her life to die a horrendous death? And lung cancer. This was seriously the coffin nail analogy someone close used to use whenever mom would light up a Camel. Yes, we are all so self-righteous when we all have reasons to point fingers at our own selves. Surely there should have been a clever comeback, but that was never one of my skills. Put that right there with power tools.

But all matters aside, I recalled a time when mom thought she lost me. I was a teenager and was shopping with my parents. They were at the grocery store and I slipped over to the fabric shop. As one who sewed, I was looking at patterns and lost in my world. Normally, I would make it back to my parents before they missed me, but this time I was so engrossed that time got away from me. Next thing, mom was standing there with her beautiful blue eyes, tears rolling down her face. She feared something happened to me.

Fast forward to that evening in 1988 when my green eyes were pouring incessantly, bleeding out from my heartache. I thought I had lost her. I wish I could say that it was not true, but I lost her. It was about six months later when she took her last breath. And the next time I would cry was when they closed her coffin. She was gone. My other brother was there to comfort me. And now, I rarely ever cry. Could I have lost all those tears, knowing nothing is worse than that time when she was forever to be gone?

I say all this to say. It is okay to hurt and let that hurt pour out from your chest. Cry. Shout. Release. This is more than likely going to happen in all our lives. You are not alone.

Thelma Tomey

Colors of Time

I can choose my dreams destiny
though they may have gathered dust
brush away remnants of shame
as I move forward into the glance of light
I study the corners that emit the white light, past the
cobalt, crimson, piney shadowed green, amber glint
on the disc of the spinning
wheel
the projector forces the light
when I focus on before
my memories with their colors of
blue, red, yellow
I realize just how much I have grown
how much I have found the gentle
nurture in fleeting moments of time
how when I stop and free the colors to merge
as they find a new name
they are no longer defined, but exist
then, and only then can I understand
the truth, the beauty, of the colors of time

I Will Choose Peace

You will end this day
both shoes on the floor
bare toes stretching to the foot board
comfy pillows under your head.

What's the point of complaints
when your state of mind
takes away
from that one possible moment of Zen.

Blink and you miss it, they say.
I say blink and forget it.
Let that one soft breeze
flowing through your screen
comfort you.

Too much time spent
to idly suffer
leaves less time for laughter.
Leaves less time for joy.
Leaves less time for peace.

If you read this up to this point
then I expect your dreams will be
a bit more honey
a lot less grumpy.

Signed, Your Peace Turtle

Author's note: As one who has had depression much of my life, I fully realize that it is not so simple to not feel depressed. What this poem suggests is to give this one time, this one moment as a gift to yourself, to provide even a brief period of peace.

Previously published in *The Literary Parrot: Series 3* (2022)

Pies

Mom was a talented baker of pies
I celebrated when I would arrive home from school
there would be cream pies cooling on the dining table
the scent of vanilla and crust would greet me at the door

Anticipation would wait until after supper
when slices of sweet banana custard with mile high meringue
teased my sweet craving tongue and slithered into a happy
tummy

She cooked from scratch, but kept a recipe handy
spotted from years of use
Crisco, white flour, a pinch of salt and this and that
she coaxed the crust into mounds, aggressively rolled
over flour covered waxed paper
eased it into tins
while she sang a country tune
stirred the sweet, vanilla scented pudding
layered it into the pie shell with bananas

After the preparation of at least three pies
she would whip up meringue, best remember cream of tartar
piled dollops to peaks and a short oven toast to the end

It was rare when I could watch mom bake
she liked a least interrupted kitchen, much like I do

How I wish she were here
she would not have to bake pies
I would simply love to hear her sing her songs
and hear her stories of long ago

Mom's Custard Pie

3 eggs, beaten
½ cup sugar
¼ teaspoon salt
3 cups milk, scalded
1 teaspoon vanilla
dash nutmeg
unbaked pie shell

Oven 425°
In a large mixing bowl, stir eggs, sugar, and salt together.
Gradually add scalded milk and mix well. Stir in vanilla.
Pour into pie shell. Sprinkle with nutmeg.
Bake 40 minutes or until knife inserted near rim comes out clean.

I love that this is an easy recipe and uses common ingredients.

Mom's Boston Cream Pie

Mom made this often. It is one of my personal favorites.

1 tablespoon shortening or butter
½ cup milk
1 cup flour
1 teaspoon baking powder
½ teaspoon salt
2 well-beaten eggs
1 cup sugar
1 teaspoon vanilla

Oven 350°

Boil water in the bottom pan of a double boiler. Place the top pan atop and add shortening to milk and stir until shortening melts. Combine flour with baking powder and salt. Beat eggs well and add sugar. Gradually add vanilla, then slowly add the milk/shortening mixture. Once well mixed, add the dry ingredients and blend thoroughly. Pour into either 1 prepared round cake pan. Bake 25-30 minutes until tested as cake done. Cool cake and split layers.
Fill layers with Custard Cream Filling (recipe follows).

Custard Cream Filling

¼ cup sugar
2 tablespoons butter
¼ cup flour
2 eggs, well beaten
¼ teaspoon salt
1 ½ teaspoon vanilla
2 cups milk

Mix sugar, flour, and salt in top of a double boiler. Start the water in the bottom pan to boil. Slowly add milk, stirring while cooking until thick (like gravy). Cover and cook 10 minutes. Add butter and eggs and mix quickly. Cook 1 minute. Cool and add vanilla.

Place one of the halved layers of cake on a plate and spread entire custard filling over the layer. Place the other half layer over the filling.

Use a simple chocolate glaze or frosting over the top.

Refrigerate.

Remedy

there has to be a remedy
for loneliness
perhaps a puppy
or a kitten
but not everyone
can have a pet
a stuffed animal
for this grown man
well, I just don't know
if he would like that
a note card with a poem
a letter signed with love
a phone call, please speak up
a visit with a lot of hugs
a peck on the cheek
whatever it takes
to make him smile
he told me he is alone
he told me he is sad
he told me he is lonely
remedies mean so much
for whatever ails us

now, to find the answer
to help this elderly man
feel happy
a remedy for sadness
priceless

Sister Movies

I put on her movie top today
it's white with blue flowers
the one she wore on Fridays
when we would go
to a sister movie
it could be a sappy romance
Bollywood flicks
Jane Austen movies
anything sisters might watch
we'd watch the previews
oh, that's a sister movie
we would say together
and plan for when it would
be ready for us to watch
if the movie lacked luster
we'd whisper about this and that
Friday mornings
I still get the urge
to gather my money
and wait for my sister
and go to a sister movie
how I miss those times

followed by frozen custard
and a ride about the town
before coming home
to relax some more
Fridays should be officially
sister movie days
but I would have to borrow yours

Previously published in *Jane Austen, an anthology of thoughts & opinions* (2021)

Paula's Chocolate Sheet Cake
A family favorite

Sift together: 2 cups flour, 2 cups sugar, 1 teaspoon baking soda
Boil: 2 sticks butter, 1 cup water, 4 tablespoons cocoa
Combine all of the above ingredients and mix well.
Mix in: 2 eggs, ½ cups buttermilk, 1 teaspoon vanilla, 1 small can of chocolate syrup (8 ounces)

Prepare a large sheet cake pan. Pour completed mixture into pan. Bake for about 35-45 minutes. This cake will be super moist. It should test clean when done.

Ice with your favorite chocolate frosting while cake is still hot.

This is Not a Poem

This is not a poem
from the moment I lay in the warmth of her womb
protected from the world--I felt her love
the songs she sang and the way she walked
carrying me within I knew I was loved
This is not a poem
but an anthem of sorts
When I entered the world
the air touched my face and I cried
she was the first to hear
this is not a poem
it's a record one could say
mom used to tell the story
of my birth day every birthday
of how she counted my fingers and toes
and I was her beautiful child
this is not a poem
it is the closeness of my mother's heart
and the iambic pentameter
of her heartbeat

Previously published in *Heart Beats, anthology of poetry* (2021)

The Best Caregiver, Ever

A few years ago, I had knee replacement surgery. It was a major decision, supported by the fact that my knee no longer served my needs. In preparation, I stocked the cupboards and bought several quarts of egg drop soup from our favorite restaurant. As I was the only person in the household who drove, I needed to be certain that we had everything we needed.

My adult daughter was to be my caregiver, assisting me with my basic needs, including watching me walk, just in case I tumbled. Fortunately, I was able to provide for my own personal care, but with being on strong medications it was best that I did not try to cook.

I had a sofa sleeper and we kept it open as I would be napping as I healed, so it made the most sense. My daughter stayed with me and woke up when I woke, even in the middle of the night, to make sure I had my walker when I would go to the bathroom.

Every morning, she made my coffee. Then, she cooked us breakfast. As I readied for physical therapy, she helped tidy up and made sure there were no obstacles.

I counted my pills, not to give her this task, and recorded my intake, so my more tired mind did not forget and take too many. Some things you have to care give for yourself and maybe even save someone else the feelings of guilt although mistakes happen. It helped me a lot to keep a chart. It also helped to pre-medicate for physical therapy.

When the in home physical therapist came, my daughter went upstairs to take care of her needs and have some alone time.

She was there with me most of the time and I needed her. Sometimes I felt guilty because my mother said that a child should not have to care for their parents. Thing is, she was no longer a child. She was an adult and volunteered for adult duties. Besides the perks of watching TV shows together, we enjoyed each other's company.

My friend came by with fancy coffee and ran some errands for me. She and my daughter are also friends and she took my daughter with her. I wanted her to have a break, so she didn't burn out. And when opportunities came for her to go and do with others, I pushed her to get out and do.

She care gave to me well enough for me to get by on my own. And, as sure as I write this, I have had the opportunity to care for her right back, not an owing, but a being, the best human way.

When Love is At Stake

You cannot go in
and sit by the bed
hold a hand
give a hug
kiss whenever you wish

You cannot go in
and be there for them
as many as can be there
you cannot be one
they must be alone

This creature that harms
has taken great hold
as much as you love them
you must know
only communion of souls

Take a seat in the car
keep your phone fully charged
eat what you can
and coffee your cup
waiting for the call

Trusting in others
is a hard thing to do
yet we are forced
to make this a choice
when love is at stake

Previously published in *TAF Stays Home* (2020)

I Remember

In times of trial
I remember
to watch for the ones
who can offer the help
to be there for others

Having survived diseases
having survived hurricanes
having survived the many storms of life
always there were helpers
to soothe the weary souls

Be aware of the people
who can take the time
who know what to do when tried
and maybe
just maybe be one of them

Previously published in *TAF Stays Home* (2020)

Angels Walking Among Us

As we sat in hospice
there were unexplainable things
spirits, I guess you could call them.
She saw them
they were calling her home.
That is why they call it homegoing
there is no home coming to you.
Her eyes were closed
as I played music to soothe her,
but angels had their own band playing.
I am sure their music cancelled mine.
When the nurse came by, I asked about these things.
She said that all kinds of things would happen
in all of hospice
they were waiting on souls.
And it came to me on that night
you did hear their music.
You did hear the call to go home.
It was not long before you took that call.
You entered the hallways.
Your feet were not touching the floor.
Your arms were not feeling IVs.
You had no more suffering.

He Knew Where to Find Home

Shannon slept alone
staying in the shed
by the back porch
this was his home
he knew the evening sounds
were there for solace
he knew they were there
to offer him company
and yet alone
he slept-and had this thing-you know
where comfort found him
when life was closing inward
when voices called his name
he had a place to go where
life kept him alive
and he did not know
why he breathed
not the gin nor vodka
not the burn of drugging
not his mother
who breathed for his life
it was nothing and it was
everything that moved back
and forth into his tired soul
now, when he walks by

there is no imprint of soles
because now he walks
in the twilight of the night
and lives on the other side
finding his final resting place
his home

Previously published in Warren Artist's Market Annual Anthology, *The House I Lived In.* (2020)

Heartbreak

When I was 44
the possibility of birth
blindsided me
all these years
I tried with no success
thinking it was a no
there you came
and I welcomed you
all of age I worried
knowing I needed
to keep you alive
self-love became essential
for baby love of you
and care I did
no caffeine
no shellfish
and lots of fruit
all I wanted was fruit
and you
when the technician
called you a speck
I was heart hurt
you are not a speck
you are a soul

Previously published in *Blogoverse*

Hearts to Hands

As you lay in the hospital bed I was lost.

You were jaundiced, dying, and needing care.

You looked into my eyes:

"my feet are cold"

Gently placing my hands on your feet,

feeling the thin parchment like skin,

and observing the golden glow of jaundice.

Mixing Vaseline with hospital lotion,

then warming the mixture in my hands.

Massaging your soles, arches,

and rounding to the dorsum

such warmth flows, energy exchanges.

Stretching each toe, kneading the pads, some pop.

Our smiling eyes connect as softness pervades.

Warming your fuzzy slippers on the heater,

scrunching and easing them on your warm, softened feet.

Just standing with hands on your covered feet,

having a private moment,

energy pouring from my hands and exchanging hearts.

How I wish that moment would heal you.

Even if a new day meant another treatment.

Each day is the chance to show you how much I love you.

I do and you love me too.

Words did not have to be said.

I knew it when you looked at me and said,

"my feet are cold."

Previously published in *Fine Lines Literary Journal*

Last Call for Boats Parker

Harvey Parker ambled his way into his room at the assisted living facility. He saw the prominent package sitting on top of his chest of drawers.

"Holy crap! What a damn place to set this box. Why not just tell everybody I have to wear these damn diapers? What the hell?" He looked at his roommate, who remained staring at the TV. "Hey, are you listening? How come they left these here?" And with this, Harvey took his cane and whacked the box of adult diapers and knocked them on the floor. He then kicked them out to the hallway and slammed the door. Harvey plopped down on his bed and felt a rush he could not help. He wet his pants.

"Time for clean-up. Men, head to your stations for maintenance. There may be several days before we restock. I'm not sure we have ample supplies to make it to the next seaport. Let's get a count going." Harvey, the Boatswain's Mate, or "Boats Parker" gave out his orders to make sure that everything was, well, ship shape. His chief concern was that there be sufficient supplies and food on hand so his shipmates could make it before the next port. The war was heating. They never knew when they would make it to a safe place to reload.

"Gaah! I need another diaper. Hey, Pete, I need another one of these God forsaken things. Can you toss me one?" Harvey's roommate, Pete, retrieved the box of diapers from the hallway and opened it. He cracked the bathroom door and tossed

Harvey a diaper. Harvey caught it like an angler reeling in a catfish, barely touching his fingers, but good enough. "Thanks, pal. You are all right." Pete just shook his head, grumbling, and plopped down on his chair and turned up the TV.

Keeping watch through four-hour rotations, Harvey listened as the waves crashed against the ship. Sitting under the gun turret, he kept a stern eye on potential enemy invasions. His job was serious, and he would let nobody down. Harvey was among many unsung heroes. He made sure, along with his shipmates, that there would be plenty of notice if there was any potential encroachment on their domain. These were scary waters, not safe from invasion, where each boat had an owner based on the country. His boat was from the USA and he was a proud Navy man. Harvey's eyes showed no fear. He only saw purpose and fulfilling that purpose. He would not do more or less than belly up to the bar, only after the fact, only after it was over. Then, and only then, did he let down his guard. Even then, it was not a powerful release. Harvey had to be alert. He chose a respectable profession, dedicating his life for every single minute, every single day of his career.

"They make these things out of tissue paper; I swear they do. Another way of taking my money. Aargh, it's aggravating. Hey, Pete, are you still there? I need another one of these cheap rags. This one's falling apart." Pete sat glued to the loud TV. Harvey looked to his side and yanked the string. In came the nursing assistant, who found Harvey sitting on the toilet, with a wad of toilet tissue in his hand and his diaper on the sink. "There's something wrong with this thing," Harvey said to the nurse. "I can't get it to work. I think it's broken." The nurse sighed and took the diaper, straightened it out and helped Harvey put the diaper on. "Thank you, honey." And after he was situated, Harvey went to his bed and took a nap.

Moving in the narrow passageway, Harvey made his way to his bunk. Harvey climbed on the top level, stacked three cots high, and passed out. Well, as much as a sailor could pass out in the war zone. It was more like catching a few winks with one eye open. Harvey trusted his men to keep watch, but just the same, you never knew if the enemy might surprise you. There were others who were sleeping, those who also stayed up all night, in their watch stations. Between farts and snores, it was musical splendour, never to replay without lots of failures. Some things bore no need for repeating.

One Saturday, Harvey was sitting at the kitchen table. He was putting all his pills in one of those medicine boxes. His wife, Virginia, had regularly taken care of this, but she passed away about a month prior. His granddaughter had already organized them. Harvey thought the medicines were unsorted, so he tried to organize them. He took his bedtime pills and retired early that night. The next morning, Harvey was more tired than usual. He was invariably a little tired and achy in the mornings. He tried to get out of bed, but he fell on the floor and cracked his head on the night table. That would have likely been to his demise if his daughter had not gotten concerned when she did not get her daily call from her dad.

"All hands-on deck!" Harvey and all others on the battleship ran to their stations. Harvey's was under the gun turret. The enemy was firing. An explosion was so loud that Harvey lost his hearing for a moment. He manned his station and fired with all he had. Sweating and cold, Harvey and his shipmates assessed the damages and the losses. They took all the injured for treatment and secured all who died for their next journey.

Waking up in the hospital emergency room, Harvey looked around. He knew where he was, but he did not know why. His daughter and son were sitting in the room and rose to his side.

"Dad," his son, Henry spoke, "You tumbled and hurt your head. And you had too much medication in your blood. They think you overdosed on your pills." Harvey tried to rise from the bed, but it was like a weight was holding him down. They strapped him to the bed, he learned, for his own safety. His face greyed, and he lost his expression with the realization that he may be in trouble.

Harvey and the crew rigged a commendation ladder and transferred temporary caskets to boats, which would take them to another location for a shallow burial. Harvey was the Boatswain's Mate and as the side boy he piped them over to the side with the long devotional Boatswain's Call. This was the protocol.

"Is it time for my last call?" Harvey asked, looking at his children with the most serious, if not determined eyes. "Sounds like I messed up. And I don't want to be a burden." Then his daughter spoke up, wiping the tears from her eyes.

"No, Dad, you are not going anywhere." And that was when they decided. Harvey would have to move to an assisted living home. He would have a roommate because he did not have the money for a private room. The doctor assured him it would be for the best so he would get his medicines taken care of and be safer. That Harvey had bladder cancer, well that was another reason.

"Harvey, my God, how I have missed you," his wife, a young, redheaded, green-eyed beauty, greeted him. They kissed and put their arms around each other, walked to the platform and caught the train back to their apartment. They had gotten married after Harvey joined the Navy, and when they bombed Pearl Harbor, everything moved to high speed. There was work to do on the military end and the honeymoon was short, just long enough to conceive Rebecca. When they got to their apartment, Harvey's mother-in-law and his daughter were waiting for him. The first time he laid eyes on Rebecca, it was love at first sight. His girl would not have to worry about being separated from her father again.

Rebecca was sitting in Harvey's new assisted living accommodation. She surveyed the environment after she put his things away.

"Dad, it looks nice here. I think you will like it and having a roommate, well, maybe you won't feel so alone. We'll come to see you often and you call if you need anything. We'll always be here for you, in a heartbeat." Harvey looked around his room, his heart in his throat. He coughed in reflection. He tried to be strong, but his eyes were leaking.

"I will never leave you again, Rebecca. Your dad finished the military and will always come home every day. I look forward to seeing you waiting for me when I get home."

Rebecca's heart was full of happiness, and she looked forward to having her father home. After all the years he was away, she did not know him and vice versa. Harvey did his best to find work after he got out of the Navy. He got a job as an insurance sales agent and tried to sell a policy to an Air Force recruiter. His job was not going so well. He had been working for commissions, and there was not anything else in prospects.

Harvey mulled over what to do. When he learned from the recruiter that the Air Force was often less likely to keep him away from family for exceedingly long, Harvey joined the Air Force. When he got home, after enlisting, he told his wife and she looked at Rebecca.

"I know what you are thinking, honey, but you two will have me around more often. It's different in the Air Force. We may have time apart, but I won't stay gone for long periods, unless a war takes me away." Hearing his own words, Harvey felt regret, but he recognized he needed to provide for his family. At least he knew military protocol, so a distinct branch could not make that much difference.

"Rebecca, I was thinking about when I told you I would never leave you when I joined the Air Force. Do you remember that?" Rebecca nodded to her father. "Look how that turned out. I didn't get to see you for over a year when they transferred me overseas. I guess I am just worried that you'll go somewhere, and I'll be alone. Your brother will come see me, I am sure, but either way, I could lose one of you." As soon as he said all this, Harvey felt awful. He did not want to guilt his children. He was just so nervous that his stomach ached. Harvey decided to just leave it alone. "Well, I am sure everything will be okay. I look forward to seeing you all when you can make it. I love you."

While Harvey did not get in on the baby stages of Rebecca, he did with Henry. He helped his bride when he got home each night. He fed Henry his bottle and changed his diapers. This was his way of giving his companion a chance to have time for herself and for him to bond with his children. Rebecca enjoyed her father being home each night until he joined the Air Force. He was away for a while for specialized training, then he was home until they sent him to Europe. After a year, Virginia, Rebecca, and Henry joined Harvey in Germany and they that was the last separation. It all worked out, and Harvey retired from the Air Force.

Harvey woke up from his nap with a wet diaper. He went to the bathroom. He was so confused that, once again, he had to call for help. The nurse was kind to him and assisted him with his fresh diaper.

"When will this all end?" Harvey asked the nurse. She sighed and helped him get cleaned up for dinner. "I'm not hungry, honey. Do you think I could rest a little longer?" The nurse nodded in agreement, knowing Harvey could not hear her well. He lost most of his hearing. A war injury, he said. Harvey took another nap in his easy chair.

They rigged the commendation ladder and lowered Harvey's casket for a shallow burial. Harvey listened as the side boy piped them over to the side with the long devotional Boatswain's Call. This was the protocol.

Previously published in *The Knob*

Aunt Alta

they crossed borders
it was a creek
it was a river
it was a shadow
it simply was whatever it was
that had to be crossed to get to here
and it was long after the crossing
when this pioneer became my own
when the genealogy of love
drew blood together
and offered hope
offered a mentor
offered an inspiration
to this young soul
always older than her sweet smile
yet, her youth showed in those moments
of such sweet sadness turned to life
and it was when she and I held company
over packaged cookies and evaporated milk
that we bonded
and it was in the fabric of her quilts
where I gave my part, to keep heritage going
her heart is imprinted in every cloth I stitch
my dear Aunt Alta

Sergeant George

Tears graced his cheeks. Broken down by the loss of yes, another girlfriend, my best buddy was in pain. "I will marry you when I grow up," my heart filled throat promised. Marrying him seemed doable to me, the six-year-old to his 36. Sergeant George was my best friend.

"I feel so sad for Sergeant George," mother's blue eyes glistened. "When it comes to women, he has one problem. He bugs them, won't leave them alone. Once he has a girlfriend he hangs at her doorstep as soon as she gets home. If he played hard to get, he might keep a woman." Mother could relate, as this is what our father did with her. He showed up everywhere she was. She said she married him so he would leave her alone.

Friends become family in military life. When our baby brother was born, we were all farmed out to different homes. When he needed surgery, having four kids at home was an issue. Sergeant George took on us kids. My toes felt a surge of excitement.

A food enthusiast, Sergeant George put menu planning first. His famous blueberry pancakes were to be the big event. Enlisting my older brother's help, they made pancakes. Stomach growling from the aroma, all set for a plate, and imagine confusion. "Where are the blueberries?" I asked. Sergeant George realized he forgot. "It's okay." Appealing to him, "We can put them on top." And he smiled.

The military transferred us to Texas. We never saw Sergeant George again. Eventually, he retired from the Air Force and moved in with his mother. Here is the thing, though, with military life. When you make close friends, they become your forever family. Mother was a big letter writer and I followed in those footsteps. I would write Sergeant George. Occasionally, he would call. Whenever I talked to him, we always ended the call with my promise I would marry him one day, ending the call with tear choked goodbyes.

Sergeant George became ill with diabetes. At the young age of 60 he left this world. That special bond, I have never felt for anyone. He was my knight, who I trusted. I still tear up to think of his loneliness. Whenever I feel lonely, I am reminded that there was this man who would always love me, no matter what.

She

She's hot, she's looking great! She is all dolled up, so to speak and that special date is just around the bend. When...wait for it...pain sets in. Her head starts a slight pressure, and she knows what is next. But. She waits. Then the signs start coming on more and more. She slowly goes to their room and slips off her fancy sandals, you know, the ones with the gold trim that show off her pretty feet. There's no going out tonight. She slips off her pretty dress, the one with the sexy cleavage and pulls off her underthings. When she has her comfortable, soft gown on, only then does she accept that this is for the moment. She holds on to hope that the next time she will at least get to the car before she feels it, once again. And maybe, just maybe, she will make it to the restaurant. She might get to have a meal with her beloved. It is a hope. And she holds on to that.

She must have hope. She finds some way to muster up a smile and more courage to face another day. She apologizes once more to her beloved, because while he knows and understands, she needs to say the words. She is sad when she thinks of how many times, she has had to change her plans. He truly does understand.

He helps her get comfortable with a fresh ice water and her medications. He may have to give her a shot. He may need to stay with her while she drifts off. Or he may need to leave her alone and make the room as dark and cool as possible. This is when he is her knight in shining armor. Well, you could say that is most of the time. He is always her lover. He is always her best friend. This is called what love is all about. And he knows.

They hold each other's souls. They hold each other's hands. They hold each other's hearts. This is true love. It anybody is lucky enough to have this, that is wonderful. And it happens. It happens not just with two committed souls like these two. It happens with friends, outside of the romantic realm. It happens with family, the kind who care. It happens. And for those it doesn't happen for. What do you say? Well, if you are aware, guess what...that is you.

Silence

The morphine drip is shielded
Hidden from plain sight
Tucked away in her nest
Snuggled under fresh covers
No pain, no worries
Just solemn slumber
Taking a cue from her
I push my recliner close to her bed
I press my body close to her side
Taking her hand, I close my eyes
And enjoy peaceful slumber
This is the supreme closeness we need
Hers to know she's not alone
Assurance as she grasps my hand snuggly
As much as I grasp hers
And rest we must
Her for relief of pain
Me for energy restoration
And we sleep

Previously published in *The Sound of Brilliance: The Short of It –
Volume 1* (2021)
Nominated for the Pushcart Prize

Stairs of Life

ascents and descents
stairs are a lot like life
with ups and downs
taking first steps
cajoling along the way
making sure your child is safe
once they are alone
taking their own steps, choices
going up and down
how we want to be there and hold
hands out like we're banisters
letting them go free
is one of the toughest things
but oh, so vital
to watch their independence
wishing they would hold your hands
holding them in hearts
keeping watch and being there
just enough to show
they have got this, and they know
you are going to be there
then there comes a time
when you're not so much around
when they're on their own
and you trust that all you've done
is enough and hope it's true

and before you know
they are helping someone else
crawling up those stairs
holding hands and guiding them
it's the circle of dear life
when you are the one
who needs help as you ascend
trusting they will be
holding you close in their hearts
and the world moves at your pace
you will know the life
as the descent comes for sure
where the light still shines
from the glow of your most dear
as you make that final climb

The Turning Point of Letting Go

Once the tone of the call vibrated
distress filled their hearts
they knew deeply this was it
the end was close

It is time to release this soul to journey
to places green and free
suffering no more

Letting go is love
she loved you then
she loves you now only more

When the one you love suffers
Is it not better to release
let them know their freedom
of no more worries
is that not the best

After all, she gave her all
so you would have life
now it is her turn to go
and dance with her beloved

To dance again in the clouds

When you left
it was as it the earth ended.

Yet you spun off
to another place,
safe and serene
where you could breathe
inhaling the essence of peaceful slumber
before you danced
once again.

You are the dancer,
releasing all your pains
and now
you have the stage.

You have made the lifetime rounds.

And now you are healed.

We all Pitched In

We all pitched in for brother's care
Mother was the lead
We all learned what it means to share

All her words were spoken fair
Teaching us this need
We all pitched in for brother's care

Morning brought my elder brothers
Cooking him his cream of wheat
We all learned what it means to share

Baby bottles were my fare
Mother taught me how to feed
We all pitched in for brother's care

Mom was always stationed where
Guidance came to be a need
We all learned what it means to share

Mom made certain to be there
As we proceeded to meet needs
We all pitched in for brother's care
We all learned what it means to share
Previously published in *Blognostics*

What I Will Keep

Rose gardens

Carnations at the base of the roses

Tomatoes from Midwest gardens

Onions at their baby size

Potatoes fresh dug from the ground

Soups in the pot all day

Worms in the mulch

Fishing rod and reel

Water at the lake

Clay at the bank

Scents of mud and florals

Crunching of shoes on the trails

Mushrooms at the base of oaks

Treasures of branches and leaves

Nature's gifts galore

An owl at my window

Dogs at the lead

And you in my heart

When a Friend Dies
Dedicated to BB

When a friend dies
it is like your own soul
pitches for a reunion.
I found out
when I had news
to share
and they were gone.
It was no accident.
His soul found mine
as he wanted me to know
he reached the other side.
Save a seat for me BB.
We will paint pictures
and write poems
to whisper in the dreams
of the living.
For now
I will sleep
and wait for my dreams.
Muse along
my friend
muse along
and whisper in my dreams.

Blue Eyes

it was your eyes, dear brother
as clear as April rain-even your tears were beautiful
although, they were seldom
with your big sister – me – other sister & brothers
it was my day job to give you a bottle
I would hold you close to my heartbeats
even though you went to the purported
beautiful place unseen by mere earthly
inhabitants, you make that transport
to meet the place daddy would allude to in his prayers
he always asked for you to
walk and play and see like others do
you deserved more goodness in this unqualified world
little brother, kiss mom and daddy for me
I trust you have gotten to know your
oldest sister, brothers, and many others
it is a beautiful place because you are there
those beautiful blue eyes
when I see them again, I will know-I have found your soul
Previously published in the anthology: *Stories & Poems in the Song of Life*

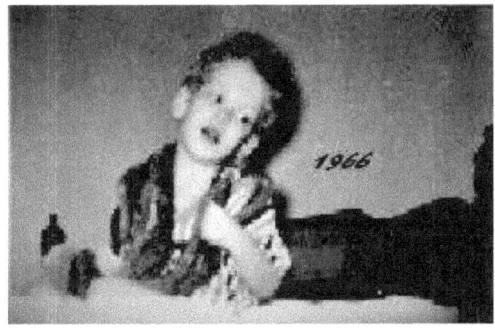

Jeffrey Keith Tomey

Brother

What can I tell?
When the owl roosts on the branch
Each night watching me as I fall to sleep
Often, I wondered
If the owl knew my thoughts
My worries
And I often thought he did
He came to visit each night
Witnessing my young teen life
And it seems he stopped by
Just when I needed some assurance
Of a life truly meant to be certain
When my heart was breaking
Because of the loss of my brother
The owl stopped by each night
To make certain I could sleep
Hearing his call helped me rest
It's odd, don't you think?
How he came by each night
Just when I needed
The presence of my brother
He came by every night

Previously published in *The Sound of Brilliance: The Short of It-Volume 1*

Compassion

take notice of pain
it comes in all kinds of ways
soulful and sadful
spiritually obscure
physically in malaise

hold close the hurting
if not in arms try in hearts
you may not know what
kind of aching may be felt
trust that caring matters more

pull the chains from souls
release viral compassion
secrets can be held
truly, passions can be shared
without conditions all known

Previously published in *Adelaide Literary Magazine*

The Last Haircut

Mounted on the back of the toilet seat, I intensely watched and listened as the gritty sounds of the razor cut through his whiskers and shaving cream, knowing not to speak while this most delicate operation took place, once completed, I was allowed to run my fingers through his damp mostly salty hair before he generously applied the tonic, magically turning more to pepper toned locks, combing his hair in place, to utter perfection, slapping on his spicy after shave, his head was complete, intact with precision and thoughtful with words of wisdom, which I took in with every living breath.

Emotions ran high when I got the call that Daddy would be on his final days, having moved away, I was at a loss, but I knew that it was in my path to get to him, no matter what, with the company of my sister, we traveled to him, with no regrets.

My eyes saw him in the hospital bed and as I wondered if he would know who I was he smiled, you see Alzheimer's had stolen some of his memory, but he gleefully told the nurse, when he saw us that "these are my daughters," which conjured up my happy.

Our brother came in with clippers and asked me to give Daddy a haircut and it was an honor to be asked to do this final task, as, you see, Daddy always liked to keep his hair cut, as long as I remember, as I always fussed about how his wavy locks would be cut away, but he always left some at the top, for his little girl, I liked to think, you know, just because it made me feel good.

Running my fingers through his thick mane, I closed my eyes in memory of all the times I did this as a child, going back in time before I was even to be known, to the times when sand and salt were his life, an old Navy soul before he chose the blue skies of the Air Force, as I felt the dampness of his locks, I knew that no memories would be clipped away as the roots of life run deep and even in the afterlife, who knows how much deeper those roots run, so memory does not have an end or maybe even a beginning.

Youth is not lost when there is a man such as my father in your life, we had the chance to learn about cherishing life, having a sense of humor, running through adventures, taking risks, valuing the essence of less, and so much more; Giving Daddy his last haircut grounded me in the roots of that life and the awareness that while it may be a simple haircut to some, it was an acceptance that no matter who would even see this haircut, that he left this world in honor, knowing he had the look of a respectable man, as he should.

Previously published in *Fine Lines Literary Journal*.

Hang a Light on the Moon

Keep a close watch
eyes glazed from lack of true sleep
it's the thing he does
to watch each breath in and out

Praise every moment
look for the signs
wonders what happens next
never coasting hope

As the moon shines like a friend
it shines to appeal his thoughts
his powers

Please hang a light on the moon
give energy
to the souls entwined here now
who knows when they will release

One thing is certain
moonlight always shines
even if not seen
if the clouds should hide the view
knowledge is the assurance
illumination
backdrops shadows 'til the dawn

Caring for Souls

knowing soothing dreams
ever comforting slumber
souls hope for another day
when days turn to end
and forever rests come forth
comfort will be there
the soul no longer bottled
broken free for true release

Previously published in *Adelaide Literary Magazine*

Kindness Calls

it's nature's call
flowering to openness
wanting your wonder

wonder brings hoping
opening the eyes widely
seeing nature's needs

kindness calls your name
taking steps to help the world
one heart at a time

Is It Me?

Is it me or do you think it so
looking at the world in my little nucleus
watching how each ebb and flow
comes together and washes to shore
the needs of our people

There's the lady in the store
the one about to give birth
sitting on a stool
as she runs the register
people asking for things
regardless of her condition
what to do to be kind?

There is this woman
who waits while groceries are rung
tapping their foot in anxiety
noting the total
trying their card, declined
what to do to be kind?

The neighbor
has kids full of energy
arms full to the car
rushes and drops things
kids laugh and run
nerves clearly frayed
what to do to be kind?

It takes a village, so they say
as the oceans of life bring needs ashore
asking ourselves the question again
what to do to be kind?

The Outstretched Hand

Sometimes, it seems that the high places are sought
in the temple of life, many want to be atop
wonder comes to mind of what can be done
for others in need, who cannot climb those stairs
the ones to the top of the temple
aren't they important too?

Seeking those in need can we not be the outstretched hand
whether they want to climb those temple stairs
or simply want to live life on solid ground
being there to offer that hand
making their life a better one
isn't that our call?

Once, as told by a wise man
seek not to go to the high places of the temple
reach out your hand to help others
be their light in life
isn't this possible?

Eyes opened to the possible
ways to help others to have a better place
isn't the way of hope?
to offer a hand
for hope, for every soul

How You Feel When You Help Someone

Once, I was told
by a mentor
when we do kindness for others
we do it for ourselves

Pondering those words
at first I was confused
I always thought
it was the compassionate way

Reflecting his words
I have to admit
it does feel good
to help someone

Supposing he's right
and likely he is
doing kindness to others
means feel goods for you

Spanish Cake

Mother made Spanish cake
Delicious cinnamon spiced
Egg white icing crunching
Sprinkled with chocolate crumbles
Senses took over the house
Moist, yet crumbly on my plate
Sweet to my tongue
Heaven has a place for this
When I have a miss mom moment
Cinnamon finds my palate

Spanish Cake Recipe

1 ¾ cups of flour
2 teaspoons baking powder
½ teaspoon salt
1 teaspoon cinnamon
½ cup shortening
1 cup sugar
2 eggs
1 teaspoon vanilla
½ cup milk
Preheat Oven: 375°F & Prepare 2 – 9 inch cake pans
Stir together flour, baking powder, salt, and cinnamon
Cream shortening until soft
Add sugar to shortening, continuing to beat
Add beaten eggs and vanilla and beat well.
Add dry ingredients to wet ingredients, alternating with milk
Beat enough to blend well
Pour into pans
Bake 25-30 minutes or until brown
Once cooled, frost with your choice of frosting. We always had egg white frosting on our cakes.
Sprinkle top of frosted cake with grated chocolate, is desired.
This was the most often baked cake, while growing up and my learning cake. Today, I substitute lower carbohydrate ingredients and I always use more cinnamon. Have fun with it and may you soon have the scent of cinnamon filling your home.

Country Blue Blanket

soft and country blue, crocheted
hand and heart into the allure
like a new heart in her life
new souls
to enter into her domain
cuddling
in the blanket
protecting and warming the skin
pink, rosy cheeks and toes of ten
turn around three times to a haze
blue light cast in her eyes, looping
leaving
gone

Adjusting Lenses

humankind's nature
often means brisking each day
keeping steady pace
what happens when it changes
when the leaves of life falter

as the elder man
finds the keys don't play as well
hears notes less clear
it's an evolvement of life
requiring tune ups often

as life slows way down
keep in mind the goodness

days when suns are high
look to the skies for hope
seek joyfulness each day

as each day is perfectly made
for any age to delight

The Red Sweater

Our roots are deep, just like my thoughts and her red sweater
Cast upon the heavens, she was gone
Always in my heart, she remains
Mother wore her red sweater almost every single day, warmth
surrounded her shoulders
When she passed into the other place, I gained
the red sweater as a memory, scented
with her essence
I left it hanging in my closet, never to be worn again, casting
spirit upon energy upon hope, forever
Leaning into the pure meaning of her life, comfort
was her mantra, forever
giving her all, loving
us, forever
Then it happened, moving
far away and many things to release, unplanned
the sweater disappeared, gone
the rubbish takers had taken it away, without
one single blessing from me, saddened
knowing that the red sweater was gone, forever
leaving memories alone, sadness
overtaking me as I knew, always
the red sweater was gone, thankful
for the spirit from the soul of love, forever
would remain mine.
This was the winning poem in the *Wolff Poetry* "Value" prompt contest.

Butterflies

to be like butterflies
before the aching of dawn
with burning desire
to soothe the soul forever
then and only then
do I truly realize
pain means life and life's terms
seeking nectar's goodness

Watercolor by Lisa Tomey-Zonneveld

Aftermath

as I balance life with what's found in loss
as I find the way to catch the feeling of smiles
I am reminded
go gentle on myself
as I am the only one who has that power over me
it's okay to be sad
it's okay to be happy
and pain is perfectly fine

as my noggin feels numb
my heart has a hole
seeping blood to my gut
it's okay to take time to heal
it's okay to admit to another soul
that my life feels perfectly wrong
and I will be all right

savage beasts rage internally
yet I press the pen to the pulp
scattering my thoughts
until the ink drops full
and spreads across the paper
creating a work of art
only I can know
only I can recognize

conversing with souls who passed
Mom knows how many times
I talked to her about the voices
the words of wisdom
and the feelings of remorse
and life allows me to have dreams
and see those who are gone
but never to be forgotten

as I see others in pain
it's so easy to see their needs
but never assume they are feeling as me
respecting their own sadness
and opening my heart
my ears
my mind
to allow other's sorrow inside

and this is how I heal
and don't feel selfish to allow this time
as life goes on only when loss is known
and honored

First Poem of Loss – from the virus

Born 1986
Died 2020
teacher 33 years old
an inspiration
loved and encouraged students
made high school days' worth it
and now she is gone
please allow her
spirit to live on in heart
in words, like the ones she wrote
in her students' lives
in the hearts of those who read
and feel the beating
of her heart
when she is on the other side
rooting for her kids
let them know
just like the break in-between stanzas
or the pause between chapters
drawing in that breath
of anticipation
leaves open the possibilities
let their lives fill in those spaces
so her words do not die

Rest in Peace, dear one

Spoiled Air Force Brats

Military time at the Pentagon

when daddy left for TDY

was our special time with mom.

Sister and I got to take turns sleeping in her bed.

We got to eat foods daddy didn't like

When he returned

he always brought us each a package

of peppermint Life Savers.

They had stripes like a candy cane.

Any thoughts of what I enjoyed

about daddy being gone

were forgotten with

one satisfied sweet tooth

Pee Wee - My Sleeping Partner

When I felt the warmth of your furry body
nestled against the blanket at the crook of my knees
I slumbered with the comfort of your presence
and knew you would protect me from the night.

As you listened to the sounds of crickets
and knew when there might be predators
I gladly woke to your wishes and let you out.

You knew even when a squirrel barked a mile away.
Just in case you needed to investigate further
plus to give the owls their entertainment
your mighty little self-ran into the night,
you commanded attention as you growled.

I miss you my dear companion.
You were an ever caring, vigilant soul.

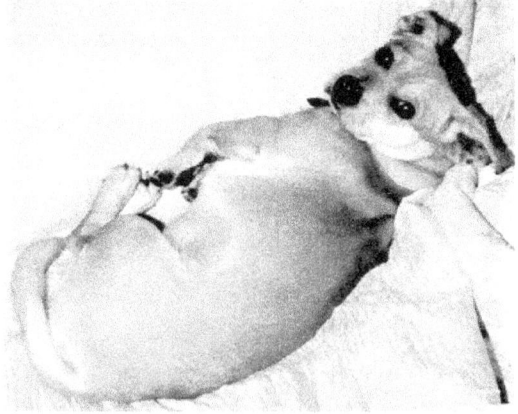

Pee Wee

Stress Management

Caregivers and receivers alike are vulnerable to stress. Stress affects health and personal relationships. If your resources to handle situations are low or depleted, there is more vulnerability to become ill or to have much confusion.

As one who has been on both ends of the caring relationship and sometimes in the middle, I fully realize that it is important to weigh out what works and what does not. These are simply suggestions. You, of course, do what works for you.

Ideally, one of the best ways to manage stress is to build an arsenal of awareness which is stocked daily. Some of the items which may help:

- Assertiveness. Practice the art of saying "no" when asked to do something which throws off your balance of energy and availability.
- Feelings Checks. Communicate about how you feel. This clears the air and helps you recognize the value of feelings. How often have we held onto certain feelings and discovered that once they are communicated, the healing begins?
- Have fun! Life is too short to spend each day without enjoyment. Take the time to play games, read, work on creative projects, play music, go to movies, or stay in for movies, go out to eat or order in, and do whatever you truly enjoy.

- Exercise. This does not mean you have to run a marathon. Go outside for fresh air, take a walk in the neighborhood, or go to a mall or gym. Senior centers offer many options to exercise and have fun. Some even have adult day programs for your person.

- Journal. Keep a journal for yourself along with encouraging the family to do the same. This provides release, insight, problem solving, and personal documentation. They also come in handy when going to medical appointments.

- Flexibility. Sometimes it seems like a day is full of compromises. When caring for others you often have to change plans to meet their needs. Accepting that each day has surprising moments makes it easier to handle whatever comes your way.

- Nutritional meals. Feed your internal arsenal to build stamina and energy stores. Treat yourself to foods you like and make meals a featured event. If able, it can be a fun activity to prepare meals with your person. Maybe they can prepare the table, wash produce, do other meaningful work, or simply stay with you as you prepare.

- Medication and Supplements. If there are medications which you must be on, be sure to take them consistently. Supplement the diet with necessary vitamins and minerals.

- Engagement. Involve your family member who has medical needs in activities you enjoy. Of course, safety first. This helps to build strong, healthy relationships. Getting others involved with activities also helps for socialization.

- Respite. Take time away from your family, if possible. Respite care could be provided by other family members or friends. If this is not possible then check into respite care programs in the community.
- Reality Checking. There are bound to be some days which are frustrating. Accepting that there are going to be these days will help you release stress. Be good to yourself. If it is a stinky day then just do your best to roll with the flow.

Activity:

On the next page, make a list of specific activities you would like to try, using these suggestions. Start small and get used to changes before pursuing more. Best Wishes.

Let's Talk About Feelings

Making a game out of feelings identification makes keeping in touch with reality fun. This can be a family event and can be incorporated into charades, as one example. Take care of yourselves and recognize that you are the most valuable resource to your loved ones. Make it fun to discover and get in touch with feelings.

Here are common feelings words & pictures.

Afraid   Angry   Annoyed   Anxious   Bored

Cheerful   Confused   Curious   Embarrassed

Excited   Frightened   Grumpy   Guilty   Happy

Jealous   Joyful   Lonely   Loving   Nervous   Proud

Sad   Scared   Shy   Sick   Silly   Surprised

Tired   Worried

This word cloud has several feelings inside. What story or poem would you like to tell using some of the words in this cloud?

Let's Talk About Journaling

Journaling helps alleviate stress and serves as a tool for problem solving. The practice of putting thoughts on paper helps the writer to sort out or list their concerns, study those concerns, and sort out possible solutions. Journals may not only have some written thoughts, but also notes or lists to the side, doodles, diagrams, whatever it takes to get through a challenge.

Benefits include sleep improvement, memory improvement, release of stress, problem solving, a lift of depression, creative flow, inspiration, and more.

Some people keep art journals with their sketches and notes to the side. Photographers may keep a journal of photos with their personal notes.

As a child, I was the one who went through the photographs and had mother tell me the stories behind these. When working with folks with dementia, these old photographs could be a tool for discussion. They may tell their stories and allow a documentation to be kept of this for posterity. This could become a living history journal.

My father told me of his stories of World War II and I recorded this and wrote a story around it. The interview was meaningful for both of us. Now, he is gone and I have a record of that event.

It is priceless. My father had Alzheimer's but was able to still go back to a time in history to tell his story. Timing, of course, was essential, but for that moment in time we were on the same page.

Some people journal every day. Others do so sporadically. I tend to journal when I am trying to problem solve. My journal is a book, but there are other times I grab the first notepad and just start writing. At my age, it is important to capture the moment. I also use my art pads as a journal, drawing and writing out whatever is on my mind.

As part of this book, I had added a few journal pages to get you started. There are no hard and fast rules, but if you are reading this book as a caregiver, it is handy to have a ready place to express yourself.

Happy Journaling!

JOURNAL

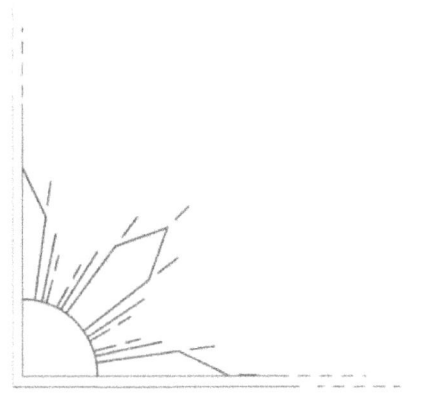

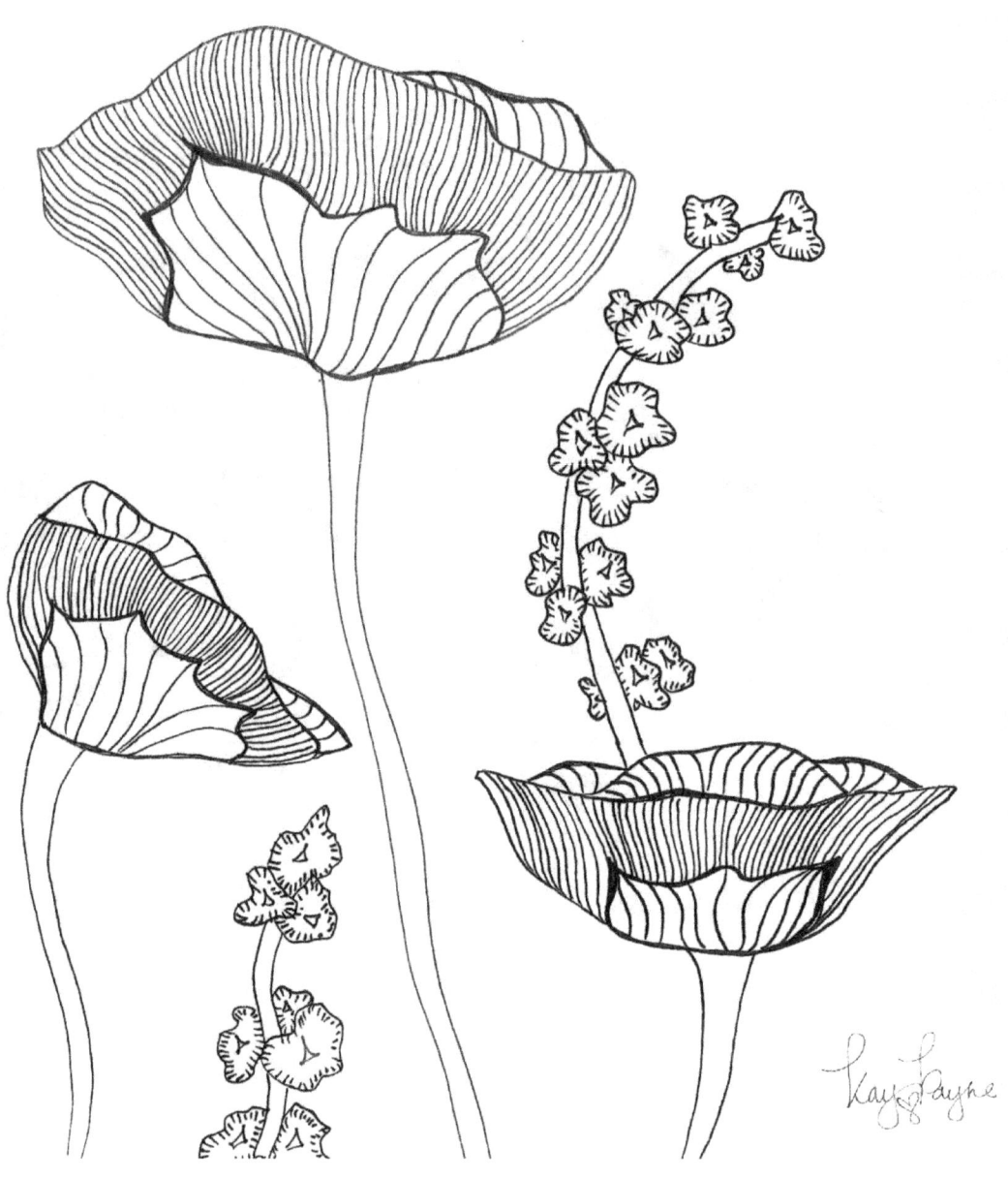

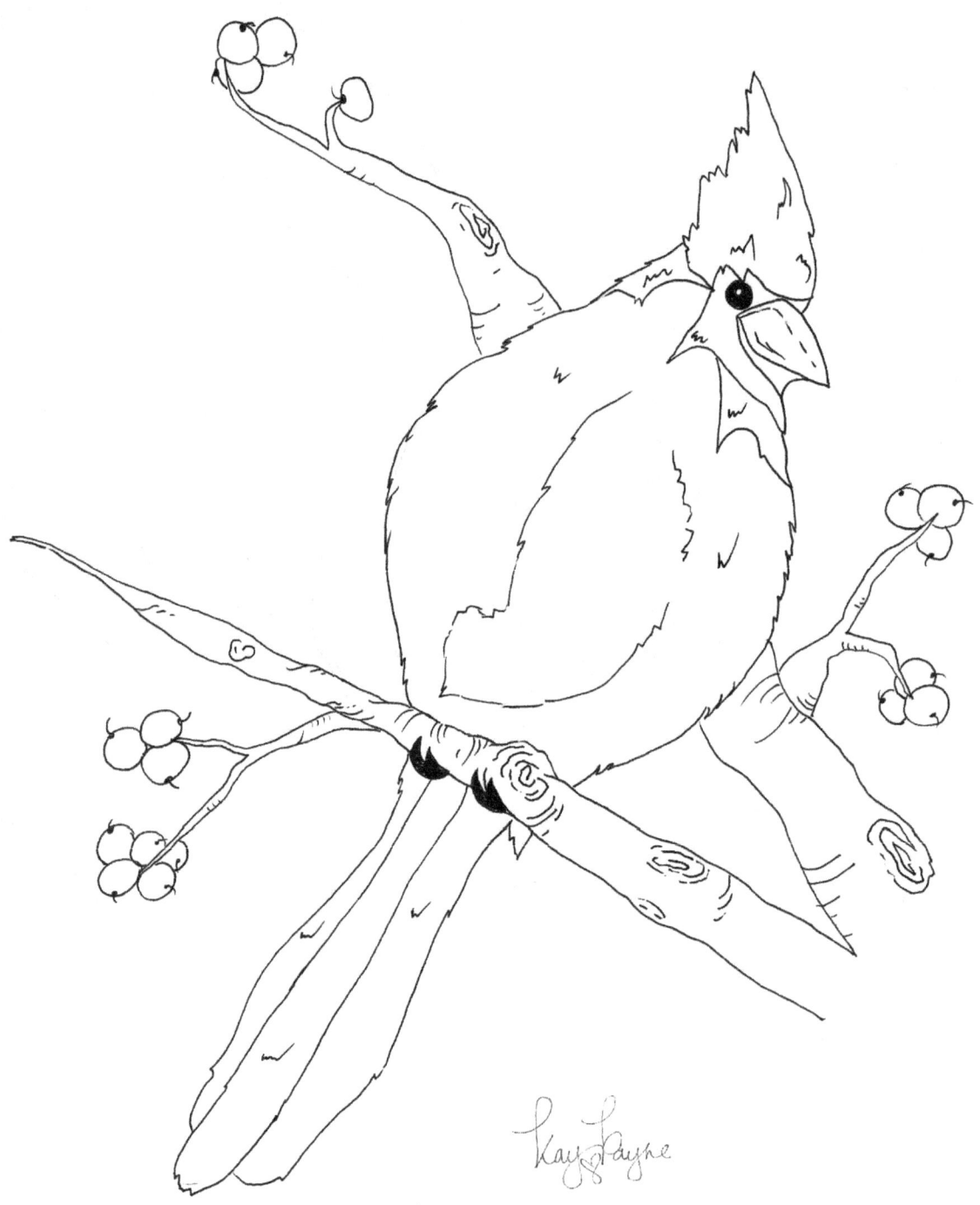

Resources

AARP The AARP.org Comprehensive resources for caregivers. You will find national and local resources for care.

Alzheimers.org.UK
Alz.org U.S. Alzheimer's Association

Caremagazine.com All things care, covers a wide range of topics to help readers with mind, body, and soul articles.

Caregiving.org Offers a comprehensive list of websites for caregivers.

CureToday.com Information about cancer.

nia.nih.gov/ National Institute on Aging

United Way First Call for Help: Dial 211 internationally for help with local resources or go to 211.org

These are just a few known resources. Within many of these are even more. Blessings and Peace to you as you search for what is needed.

Kay Payne resides in Alabama with a paintbrush in one hand and a hammer in the other. She helps her beloved with his handyman work, while raising their blended family, full of love and sweet tea.

Lisa Tomey-Zonneveld is a poet, writer, & artist from Raleigh North Carolina. She is the manager of Prolific Pulse Press LLC where she tries to get words to the world, one writer and poet at a time. She is the 2022 Poet Laureate as well as a Gold Ambassador for Garden of Neuro Institute. She is on the editing team for Fine Lines Literary Journal and a co-organizer for Living Poetry. Published works include *Silver Linings, Heart Sounds,* and numerous anthologies, including *Heart Beats* and *Social Justice Inks.* An honors graduate from Western Illinois University, Lisa has focused on Social Work as her vocation.

Thank you for taking the time to read our book of poetry, essays, art, and more. Reviews are always welcome and appreciated.

If you have any questions or comments feel free to contact: prolificpulse@gmail.com

To learn more about Prolific Pulse Press LLC go to: ProlificPulse.com